# "IF I BE A MAN OF GOD"

## GOD'S CALL TO A HIGHER STANDARD

FEMI ADUN
Author, Unlock Your Future

IF I BE A MAN OF GOD:
God's Call to a Higher Standard


ISBN: 978-1-7397009-6-6

Published by:
Gracehouse Publishing
http://www.gracehousepublishing.org

Unless otherwise indicated, all Scripture quotations are taken from the New King James Version (NKJV) of the Bible.

# TABLE OF CONTENTS

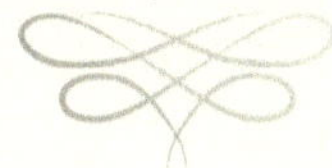

# PREFACE

The term 'Man of God' has been abused and despised in many ways over the years. Presently, it seems to not mean so much to many people, especially given our modern-day culture and Christianity. The general controversy around the subject of a 'man' or 'woman' of God has never been as intense as it currently is, and because of this, many ministers of God would rather choose to be identified by their vocation or professional title, with the hope of commanding more respect and dignity or even to demonstrate their integrity of character.

While we - as ministers of God - often find solace in this approach, we must grow a deeper concern beyond our reputation and need for public acceptance. In the Bible days, to be referred to as a man or woman of God was a thing of the highest esteem and preference. The study of the bible reveals several professionals called out of their respective vocations to bear the esteemed responsibility of being men and women of God. These men and women were outstanding stewards of the calling, which the bible refers to as a HIGH CALLING, such that respected professionals desired to even become men and women of God. Some even

offered to pay for the call! Of course, no one can buy the calling of God, but this just shows us the level of honor and dignity that came with being a man or woman of God back in the bible days.
The purpose of this book, firstly, is not to portray self-confidence or self-righteousness, and neither am I attempting to postulate that there are no true men and women of God in this current day or dispensation. To suggest such schools of thought will invalidate the revelation of this book, make me a liar, and drive us far from the truth of what I believe God has revealed to me regarding this subject matter.

The purpose and the core emphasis throughout this book are that God through His word is calling those He has called, including myself, to a higher standard. This is a standard that is only attainable through His grace and our commitment to being true men and women of God; especially in times like this when there are compromises and far-reaching skepticism about men and women of God.

Furthermore, I also believe that God, at such a time as this, is calling men and women of God to rise up in the defense of, and for the advancement of His Kingdom here on earth through every sphere of society.

This can only be achieved by a higher level of kingdom standard that is different from what we are currently experiencing in many parts of the world.

There is a sense in which we must evaluate ourselves as men and women of God similar to the Prophet Elijah in the bible. When confronted with deadly evil, Elijah boldly remarked: “if I be a man of God, let fire come down from heaven;” and according to the word of God, fire indeed came down from heaven to prove he was truly a man of God. After all, the bible admonishes us as men and women of God to walk worthy of our calling; which means, with evidence that we are truly men or women called by God.

It is biblically true that the calling of God in the life of a man or woman will remain for as long as he or she is alive, regardless of their character or lack of it. However, what is not guaranteed is the involvement of God Himself in that individual's life and ministry – just like king Saul in the Old Testament. Now, one key question on my heart as I pen down the words you will read in this book through the revelation of the Holy Spirit is this: could it be that there are actually ‘men’ and ‘women’ of God today who only just have the titles but are no longer seen by God as men or women of God?

I cannot say that I am certain of the answer to this question, as my intention as stated earlier is not to point fingers at people or posture myself as perfect. In fact, my original intent was to study the book of second Kings for my personal spiritual growth; but suddenly, during the course of my study, the Holy Spirit began to speak to me about this book with a strong sense of urgency that led me to file away an existing book project that I was getting ready to publish to focus on this.

The revelation that has led to this book is from a portion of the book of Second Kings chapter one, which is based on the life and ministry of the Prophet Elijah, who truly demonstrated that he was a man of God. It is my prayer and hope that this book will provide you an opportunity to examine yourself (as I have) and empower you to rise to a higher level standard in God, through the matchless name of Jesus Christ, Amen.

See you at the top!

# CHAPTER ONE

# THE VOICE OF GOD

*"But the angel of the Lord said to Elijah the Tishbite, "Arise, go up to meet the messengers of the king of Samaria, and say to them, 'Is it because there is no God in Israel that you are going to inquire of Baal-Zebub, the god of Ekron?'* 4 *Now therefore, thus says the Lord: 'You shall not come down from the bed to which you have gone up, but you shall surely die.' "* So, *Elijah departed".*

Being a man or a woman of God is not a self-assigned position or responsibility. To be a man or woman of God is to be called by God, which in itself, demonstrates the capacity to hear from God. Hearing the voice of God is the greatest spiritual asset a man or woman of God can possess. This is not to say that hearing from God is exclusive to individuals called by God to serve in a ministerial capacity or function within a ministry gift, as every born-again believer through the Holy Spirit has the ability to hear from God. What I am simply saying is that according to the word of God, it is not just important but necessary that a man or woman of God must be hearing from God: otherwise, he or she would have no business being in ministry or in any way defending or advancing the kingdom of God here on earth.

Samuel's ministry did not fully begin until he was able to hear from God. The Bible records that Samuel ministered before the Lord but did not know God. This interesting paradox explains why the young Samuel thought that it was his boss Eli that called him when it was indeed God trying to activate his calling as a man of God. Samuel was mightily used by God, but he first had to learn how to discern the voice of God. I am fearful for a generation of young and even some older men and women who are attempting to act on behalf of God without having heard Him. Even Jesus declares according to the gospel of John chapter five that ***He can of Himself do nothing, except what is revealed to Him by the heavenly Father. Essentially, He did as He heard from the Father***!

On several occasions, I have heard my pastor, Reverend Sam Adeyemi say, "ministry is 'God said!'", which means that the first proof that God has called you into the ministry or to pursue any kind of ministry initiative is that you have heard from God. As we see in the scriptures, Elijah did not decide to go minister to the king's messenger; God instructed him to go and speak to the messenger. You will notice that every single individual in the bible who served in the capacity of a man or woman of God did so because they heard and continued to hear the voice of God. It is dangerous to try to play the role of God's representative if you have not heard or are not hearing from God. I still think about what would have happened to Isaac if his father Abram had not heard God's command the second time to not sacrifice him, after the initial instruction from God to offer him as a sacrifice. Poor Isaac would have been a casualty of spiritual deafness, just like many innocent Christians have become casualties of so-called men or women of God who have not heard or are no longer hearing from God. When Moses showed up with a rescue plan before the people of Israel as slaves in Egypt, they immediately wanted to know if he had truly heard from God before they committed to his leadership. People's lives can be destroyed by simply following the emotions of men or women of God, instead of the voice of God.

As men and women of God, we are called to establish kingdom order here on earth, but we can only do so when we are able to hear from God. The wisdom book of Proverbs in the Bible, says that where there is no revelation, people are cast off restraint. This is true of every place where the voice of God is no longer being heard. The voice of God is the providence for every need of humanity and society. When Eli the man of God was hearing from God, the nation prospered under his leadership; but a time came when he could no longer hear God and the result was chaos all over the nation. The fearful thing is that an individual can still be referred to as a man or woman of God even when they are no longer hearing from God! Apart from the damage such a person will cause, there will also be no fruits of kingdom nature to their ministry.

## COMMUNION WITH GOD

The secret to hearing from God is to be in constant communion with Him. Prayer and fellowship of the Spirit are key; there is no other way. Period! If Jesus arose very early every day to commune with God to fulfill His responsibility as a representative of God here on earth, then you and I have no alternative means to fulfill our responsibilities as men or women of God.

Millions of people around the world got to know of the man of God called Billy Graham because he was mightily used by God for several years before his recent passing. Billy Graham clearly heard from God otherwise it would have been impossible to defend or advance the kingdom of

God in the magnitude in which God granted him. However, to my surprise, from reading his book 'Nearing home' which he wrote at 93 years of age, Billy Graham mentioned that one of the things he would have done more is to spend more time with God. What a remarkable man of God! No wonder God trusted and used him beyond every possible imagination of man.

The Psalmist declares in the 113th chapter of the book of Psalms that he would praise the name of the Lord right from the start of the day all the way to the end of it. David was a man of communion with God. He was so committed to being in tune with God. He did not joke with hearing from God, and because of this, he became a very mighty man of God. He defended and greatly advanced the kingdom of God during his reign as the king of Israel.

I am firm believer in building structures and systems to help facilitate the fulfillment of our God-given ministry vision. I have seen what a ministry can become and achieve through a solid structure and system, and I encourage every man or woman of God to learn how to put together a proper structure and system in your ministry organization; otherwise, you will frustrate the grace of God upon your life. However, more importantly, the challenge that the Spirit of God is placing before us in this current time is to develop a stronger commitment to our devotional life. Our communion with God must not come after structures and systems. God wants to be in constant daily communion with those of us that have accepted the responsibility to be His representatives here on earth.

The danger of success that we must shield ourselves from is the lack of time for fellowshipping with God. Our personal retreats should not be substituted for the busyness of ministry and projects. Apostle Paul said it is foolishness to start by the Spirit and end up doing ministry in the flesh. Are we still longing for the presence of God like we did when we first discovered our call into ministry? Is our first love for God still burning within us, or we have allowed it to fizzle out now that we think we have figured it out and are doing well in ministry?

Fellow servants of God, we are entering into a spiritual dispensation where those who have abandoned their personal altars will be clearly distinguishable from those who have kept the fire on their altars burning bright. Structural edifices, buildings, and flashing lights will no longer be the evidence and involvement of God in a man or woman of God's ministry. The acceptable standard will be those who are in unbreakable communion with God and are constantly hearing from Him.

I am seriously being challenged by a statement made by my pastor, Reverend Sam Adeyemi in his new book, ***Grace Activated.*** He wrote thus: "It is when we accept our inability to fulfill our own destiny that we recognize our deep need for prayers". I believe this is the attitude that God is calling us to have because, without this reality check, we run the risk of being men or women without God. It is time for some of us to return and for others to go deeper in our communion with God because God is longing to speak to us about our lives, His plans, and strategies but can only do so when we are listening.

We are His sheep (John 10:27), and we must be committed to His voice; otherwise, we will wander away easily and become easy targets for the predator. The truth is that we stand no chance against the craftiness of the enemy without a God-given strategy that comes in the place of listening to His voice.

As of the time of writing this book, I am a month away from celebrating 20 years of kingdom service, and I have found the prayer of inquiry to be very useful. The prayer of inquiry is an intentional act of consecration to seek direction from the Lord for the effective discharge of one's ministerial duties and obligations. In the book of 1st Samuel chapter 30, this type of prayer was clearly demonstrated by David when the

Amalekites invaded David's camp and raided it. Right in the middle of the chaos, wailing, and weeping, David pulled himself aside to seek the voice of the Lord regarding the situation, wherein lay the solution!

> *"Now David was greatly distressed, for the people spoke of stoning him, because the soul of all the people was grieved, every man for his sons and his daughters. But David strengthened himself in the LORD his God. [7] Then David said to Abiathar the priest, Ahimelech's son, "Please bring the ephod here to me." And Abiathar brought the ephod to David. [8] So David inquired of the LORD, saying, "Shall I pursue this troop? Shall I overtake them?" And He answered him, "Pursue, for you shall surely overtake them and without fail recover all."*
> - 1 *Samuel* 30:6-8 NKJV

The voice of God is not only the voice of hope or wisdom; it is also the voice of faith. It should be the driving force behind every ministry endeavor, otherwise, there is no guarantee of God's involvement, and neither can we succeed as men or women of God.

May we receive grace to go deeper with God in Jesus' name, Amen!

# CHAPTER TWO

# SPEAKING TRUTH TO POWER

"So *they said to him, "A man came up to meet us, and said to us, 'Go, return to the king who sent you, and say to him, "Thus says the Lord: 'Is it because there is no God in Israel that you are sending to inquire of Baal-Zebub, the god of Ekron? Therefore, you shall not come down from the bed to which you have gone up, but you shall surely die".*

In a time of political correctness, inclusion, and cultural sensitivity, there has never been a time such as this that God is demanding that His word should be spoken boldly and uncompromisingly by men and women of God. Did you notice that the man of God, Elijah did not change a single word in what he was instructed by God to say to king Ahaziah? Do you know what it means to tell a national leader that God said he or she will die? It is one of the most difficult messages to preach especially in today's world when you could easily be branded or arrested for treason and terrorism. But that is the standard that God is calling every man and woman of God to; not to go around speaking death to our political leaders but to stand up and speak the truth where necessary.

The times we live in presently as men and women of God demand truth based on the integrity of God's word to be spoken uncompromisingly, coupled with the soundness of our character as men and women of God. This will be the hallmark of true men and women of God in this current spiritual dispensation and political climate. God will not condole half-truths or sugar-coated truths. We are not called to make friends: we are called to make disciples. The call to change nations is not a call to make political friends. Don't get me wrong, there is nothing wrong with having friends who serve God and the nation through politics, but we must know where to draw the line as men or women of God called to speak or advise political leaders in Government. The truth of God's word should never be compromised or half-spoken because of our relationship with government officials; otherwise, we will have to answer to God.

The Apostolic responsibility of the end-time church is the reason God is giving more men and women of God access to the corridors of political powers. But the Spirit of God is clearly saying that this access to power is not for socializing or reputation building, but a sacred responsibility to stand and demand truth, righteousness, and justice. The Spirit of God is saying that anything short of this, will only jeopardize the process of kingdom invasion and the reclaiming of society from the strongholds of the kingdom of darkness.

Jeremiah's call to speak to nations as a prophet of God came with a strict warning from God to only speak as he was commanded. God's word is God; His integrity lies in it, and He won't take it lightly when we as men and women of God compromise or misuse His word.

> *"But the Lord said to me: "Do not say, 'I am a youth, For you shall go to all to whom I send you, And whatever I command you, you shall speak. Do not be afraid of their faces, For I am with you to deliver you," says the Lord.*

Like Jeremiah, God is calling us to speak the truth at all costs even when it's not popular. The church can no longer be silent and allow the forces of darkness to rule our homes, communities, and nations. The compromise of the truth weakens our effort in kingdom advancement and slows the healing process of our nations.

Let's recall these statements by Apostle Paul in 1 Corinthians 2,

> *And I, brethren, when I came to you, did not come with excellence of speech or of wisdom declaring to you the testimony of God. For I determined not to know anything among you except Jesus Christ and Him crucified. I was with you in weakness, in fear, and in much trembling. And my speech and my preaching were not with persuasive words of human wisdom, but in demonstration of the Spirit and of power, that your faith should not be in the wisdom of men but in the power of God.*

Men and women of God, this is it: this is the standard. To speak, preach, teach, proclaim, declare, decree, and prophesy God's word as it is written in God's word (the Holy Bible) and as revealed to us by the Holy Spirit of God.

Again, Apostle Paul declares, ***"For I will not dare to speak of any of those things which Christ has not accomplished through me, in word and deed, to make the Gentiles obedient"***

I believe the greatest miracles Jesus performed were the hearts He changed through the truths He taught and preached. There is nothing that beats the truth when it comes to the pursuit of transformation either at the individual or corporate level. The word of God is light and there is going to be a greater need to examine what we are listening to, and as preachers, what we are teaching and preaching. The light that shone in Peter's case was directed to the prison where he was locked up, which means we must allow the word of God into areas of people's lives where they are still being held captive. As Pastors and preachers, we must become more intentional about confronting the worldliness that people are struggling with through undiluted kingdom principles & teaching, in order for us to see supernatural breakthroughs and kingdom advancements in their lives. I believe there is going to be a greater need for discipleship within our local congregations. God's word is the antidote for every failure and the key to every human progress, and this is more reason why we cannot afford to compromise the truth as men and women of God.

> *Then the woman said to Elijah, "Now by this I know that you are a man of God, and that the word of the Lord in your mouth is the truth."*

Church leaders must come to understand that in order to be culturally relevant, no strategy or creativity will outweigh truth in this present age. The world system is gaining more prominence and power because they are no longer afraid to tell their truth. If we do not start telling our truth, we will allow the world's truth to be the only truth that this generation will know. The word of God is our truth and it upholds all things, all people, and all nations.

> *"The Spirit of the Lord God is upon Me Because the Lord has anointed Me*
> *To preach good tidings to the poor; He has sent Me to heal the broken-hearted,*
> *To proclaim liberty to the captives, And the opening of the prison to those who are bound; To proclaim the acceptable year of the Lord, And the day of vengeance of our God; To comfort all who mourn, To console those who mourn in Zion, To give them beauty for ashes, The oil of joy for mourning, The garment of praise for the spirit of heaviness; That they may be called trees of righteousness, The planting of the Lord, that He may be glorified."*

Fellow servants of God, here is my conclusion on this note as we move on to the next. It is only by the Spirit of God that truth can be told. This is why our communion with His Spirit is very vital. The Bible refers to the Holy Spirit as the Spirit of Truth, which means the more filled we are with the Spirit, the fuller of truth we will be, and the more truth we will speak.

> *However, when He, the Spirit of truth, has come, He will guide you into all truth; for He will not speak on His own authority, but whatever He hears He will speak; and He will tell you things to come.*

Truth is the standard; by the Spirit is the way.

# CHAPTER THREE

# AUTHENTICITY

> *Then he said to them, "What kind of man was it who came up to meet you and told you these words?" So, they answered him, "A hairy man wearing a leather belt around his waist." And he said, "It is Elijah the Tishbite."*

The first man and woman of God were Adam and His wife Eve; but before both of them could commence any of the responsibilities God intended for them, they had to first understand their identity in God. Adam and Eve were authentic until they sinned against God; and since then, man has battled for his/her true self.

> *So, God created man in His own image; in the image of God He created him; male and female He created them.*

In studying the Bible, you will observe that the intentions of God are clearly revealed through the knowledge of identity. King Ahaziah knew what he was up against once Elijah's identity was revealed. He knew that this was not an ordinary man, hence the reason for sending fifty able-bodied soldiers to arrest him. Unlike Elijah, our outward appearance (even though there is a place for that) is not the core of our identity as men and women of God. The core of our identity is the image of Christ in us and the calling of God on our lives, not even the spiritual offices we occupy through the grace of God.

We should not be mistaken for who we are, what we stand for, and the kingdom we represent as men and women of God. Our authority against wrong ideologies, false doctrines, or demonized systems and structures will be undermined without a solid posture of our kingdom (spiritual) identity. To stand against evil, defend, and advance the kingdom of God here on earth, we have to know who we are and who we are not.

> *There was a man sent from God, whose name was John. This man came for a witness, to bear witness of the Light, that all through him might believe. 8 He was not that Light but was sent to bear witness of that Light.*

Here is one of the reasons I admire Jesus' first cousin, John the Baptist: he knew his identity and was comfortable in what he was designed by God to be and do. John was an authentic leader and minister of the gospel; he knew he was not the Light and he did not allow anyone to talk him into feeling inferior to his cousin's calling and assignment as the Light. As men and women of God, we must become comfortable with who and what we are and are not, otherwise we would fall into the temptation of comparison and competition with ourselves, instead of collaboration and kingdom partnership. By the grace of God, I am a fivefold minister of the gospel, called with an apostolic grace to to serve within the body of Christ and nations.. It has been my responsibility to be comfortable and appreciative of this calling on my life and not think less or highly of myself other than the need to please God with my life.

My wife and I have had the rare honor and privilege to pastor a local assembly for 9 years in the beautiful city of London, England. We had the opportunity in the process to develop ourselves as well as impact many lives by the grace of God. Now that we no longer pastor a church, we now have the responsibility to oversee an apostolic outreach ministry, ***Eagle World Outreach***, which provides us the privilege of a global church oversight, empowering believers, and training ministry leaders all around the world for kingdom establishment and advancement. However, I struggled in the early stage of this transition because of the pressure and notion that I had to have a church (a big one) to make an impact or have any right to the apostolic mandate on my life.

Soon enough, I discovered through the word of God that I am simply what God says I am, and I do not need to qualify for His calling on my life by any human standard. His blood paid the price and by His grace, I am what he has ordained for me to be, not a church and not a man. Although, this does not excuse me or anyone else from the needful ministerial training and submission to God-ordained and chosen spiritual authorities as laid down clearly in the scriptures.

I have a few covenant relationships I consider as brothers and sisters in ministry and we all have different expressions of the manifold grace of God upon our lives and ministries, but we understand the need for kingdom collaboration which today has yielded enormous fruits for the advancement of God's kingdom here on earth. We can be inspired by other ministers or ministries, but God has not called us to be like others. Our desire should be to become more like Him so that we will be authentic ministers.

> *"And He Himself gave some to be apostles, some prophets, some evangelists, and some pastors and teachers, for the equipping of the saints for the work of ministry, for the edifying of the body of Christ, till we all come to the unity of the faith*

*and of the knowledge of the Son of God, to a perfect man, to the measure of the stature of the fullness of Christ".*

No race is superior, neither is any calling; we have only allowed ourselves to categorize our spiritual offices and ministries within the unrealistic measure of social class. As a man or woman of God, your image should not be based on anything external when the word of God has declared that i***t is in Him, we live, we move, and have our being***. We must stop this destructive culture of aiming to belong to an elite group of ministers from growing among us men and women of God. Elijah wouldn't have made the cut by the description of what his ministerial apparel looked like. He didn't seem to wear much on his body, yet he was fully embodied with the life of God such that he could call for fire to fall from heaven and the fire would literally fall from heaven. The same man was recorded in the Bible to have prayed for it not to rain for three years on the land, and for three years the sky held back the rain.

Elijah wasn't afraid to say he was a man of God because to be a man of God in his days was a high calling and a wonderful privilege that commanded honor from the public. I am wondering if being a man or woman of God still carries the same weight as of old, especially with our desire and false need to be seen as something else that we think may give us an accepted reputation. There is no earthly reputation that is greater than whom we are called to be and the spiritual office we are called to serve in. Jesus constantly stripped Himself of every earthly reputation, so that He could remain the man of God He was ordained to be here on earth.

I am from Nigeria, West Africa, and it is such a privilege to see what God is doing in my country of birth through the power of the gospel. The largest churches on earth right now are in Nigeria; the largest single gathering of believers is in Nigeria, and the greatest export of the gospel currently is by Nigerians. So many amazing things are happening through the power of God in the country! However, all these are not without the excessiveness and uncontrolled appetites of the human nature, which always leads to the corruption of every good thing.

Take, for instance, the following scenario: the massive influx of souls into the Nigerian church in the last era saw the need for multi-site extensions due to the long travel distances and the traffic situation of a city like Lagos, Nigeria. The city of Lagos has an average population size of 17.5 million residents, divided majorly into the mainland and the island areas with both poor and rich people. It is only reasonable to ease the burden of parishioners traveling from both ends of the city by establishing campus sites in strategic locations that are easily accessible, and for convenience of travel. However, what I observe is the opposite: an increasing notion that the 'island' ministers or churches are of a superior class that those on the 'mainland'. While this perception is questionable, it is not entirely untrue as the last 15 years of my ministry involvement in the country have afforded me the opportunity to interact with several men and women of God in the city, and this is the prevalent perception and reality that I discern, especially coming from the younger ministers.

This cultural mindset is not only prevalent in Nigeria; it is all over the world – at least in the over 25 Countries and 100 cities around the world that I have the privilege of ministry in. It is not a location thing: rather, it is the prevalent culture of the age we are living in and as men and women of God, we must be very careful not to be caught up in such division based on human classification, especially when the core of our assignment is to unite through the power of God's love demonstrated through the sacrifice of Jesus Christ. I understand that means affords us a certain kind of lifestyle, but that should not make us feel better than anyone else, especially other fellow believers. Jesus did not feel cheated or devalued to be sent into this world as the son of God in human form, so why should we class ourselves better than anyone just because of our influence or affluence?

*Let this mind be in you which was also in Christ Jesus, who, being in the form of God, did not consider it robbery to be equal with God but made Himself of no reputation, taking the form of a bondservant, and coming in the likeness of men. And being found in appearance as a man, He humbled Himself and became obedient to the point of death, even the death of the cross. Therefore God also has highly exalted Him and given Him the name which is above every name, that at the name of Jesus every knee should bow, of those in heaven, and of those on earth, and of those under the earth, and that every tongue should confess that Jesus Christ is Lord, to the glory of God the Father.*

## REDISCOVERING OUR KINGDOM IDENTITY

*"But you are a chosen generation, a royal priesthood, a holy nation, His own special people, that you may proclaim the praises of Him who called you out of darkness into His marvelous light"*

Peter in this passage points out to us his readers our identity as both believers, and as men and women of God. He tells us this for an important reason. This is very important because the foundation for the accomplishment or fulfillment (that you may proclaim) of our heavenly calling lies in the discovery of our true identity in Christ, not in the evaluations of people.

> *"Then God said, "Let Us make man in Our image, according to Our likeness; let them have dominion over the fish of the sea, over the birds of the air, and over the cattle, over all the earth and over every creeping thing that creeps on the earth."* [27] *So God created man in His own image; in the image of God He created him; male and female He created them".*

This is why from the beginning of creation, the greatest defeat in the battle for destiny, kingdom defense, and advancement is the one lost to the deception of identity, as we see from the fall of man in the book of Genesis. It is so powerful when a man or woman of God discovers and operates from their kingdom identity as therein lies the power to fulfill the dominion mandate.

## 3 BENEFITS OF DISCOVERING YOUR IDENTITY

### SPIRITUAL AUTHORITY

**IDENTITY PRECEDES AUTHORITY.** Without a true discovery of our spiritual identity, you and I will have no spiritual authority; not because it hasn't been given to us but because we cannot function in our authority as men and women of God outside of our spiritual identity. The revelation of Elijah's identity showed that the king knew him as a man of authority, otherwise he would have just sent one person to go get him instead of sending 50 of his soldiers at once.

> *And He said to them, "I saw Satan fall like lightning from heaven. [19] Behold, I give you the authority to trample on serpents and scorpions, and over all the power of the enemy, and nothing shall by any means hurt you. [20] Nevertheless do not rejoice in this, that the spirits are subject to you, but rather rejoice because your names are written in heaven."*

Also, without the discovery of our kingdom identity, you and I are unauthorized to walk and operate in the supernatural; which means, we will lack spiritual authority and be unable to demonstrate our dominion in Christ. A powerful revelation of identity that every man or woman of God needs revealed to him or her is that they have been given the power to become the sons and daughters of God. Being a soldier for Christ or a Servant of God does not give us dominion over the kingdom of darkness: rather, it is being a son or a daughter of God that confers this authority on us. A soldier is under command, a servant carries out instructions, but as sons and daughters of God we are in command and we have been given the power to instruct.

> *Now there was a man in their synagogue with an unclean spirit. And he cried out, saying, "Let us alone! What have we to do with You, Jesus of Nazareth? Did You come to destroy us? I know who You are-the Holy One of God!" But Jesus rebuked him, saying, "Be quiet, and come out of him!" And when the unclean spirit had convulsed him and cried out with a loud voice, he came out of him. Then they were all amazed, so that they questioned among themselves, saying, "What is this? What new doctrine is this? For with authority He commands even the unclean spirits, and they obey Him." And immediately His fame spread throughout all the region around Galilee.*

It is important that we know and settle this within ourselves that our authority does not come from doctrine. Instead, it comes from the revelation of who we are in Christ and through His preordained plan for our lives.

## DIVINE ABILITY

**IDENTITY REVEALS ABILITY.** What you and I can do is in who we are, and that is why, most times, the sense of inability we often feel is a function of lack of identity. Peter declares that because we are a chosen generation, a royal priesthood, a holy nation, and God's special people, you and I have been given the innate ability to outwardly proclaim the praises of God. This means that it is not what you and I can do that determines or defines who you are, but it is who we are that influences the outcomes of our life and ministry. I once heard Jesse Duplantis publicly speak about his lack of ability to pastor or grow a church, and he mentioned that it was simply because God did not design him to be a pastor! However, as a traveling teacher and televangelist, God has greatly used him to impact millions of souls with the gospel of Jesus Christ all over the world. A major hindrance or should I say 'threat' to the advancement of the kingdom of God today is ministers who have assumed mistaken identities or are under the pressure of being what God hasn't called them to be.

By the grace of God, I have been able to contribute far more to building and advancing the kingdom of God outside of pastoring than I did while I pastored a local assembly. This is not to say that there is anything wrong with being a pastor but by God's design for me, He has empowered me with a stronger apostolic anointing. We will uncover tremendous abilities and capabilities when we discover and embrace who we are in Christ and God's ordinances upon our lives.

We are all individually gifted by God, and this imbues everyone called by God with unique abilities which differ from one another. The uniqueness of my abilities or capabilities does not make me better than you or you than me. In fact, the synergy of our unique abilities makes us far better and more productive for kingdom advancement. It is important for men and women of God to understand that the uniqueness and diversity of our giftedness and abilities should not lead us to operate in silos in our interactions and efforts in defending our faith and advancing the kingdom of God.

The Apostle Paul wrote extensively about this subject to educate the believers and ministers at Corinth to understand that the Holy Spirit works uniquely in us but it's the same Spirit at work in all of us for the same God.

1 Corinthians 12:4-12 NKJV

*There are diversities of gifts, but the same Spirit. [5] There are differences of ministries, but the same Lord. [6] And there are diversities of activities, but it is the same God who works all in all. [7] But the manifestation of the Spirit is given to each one for the profit of all: [8] for to one is given the word of wisdom through the Spirit, to another the word of knowledge through the same Spirit, [9] to another faith by the same Spirit, to another gifts of healings by the same Spirit, [10] to another the working of miracles, to another prophecy, to another discerning of spirits, to another different kinds of tongues, to another the interpretation of tongues. [11] But one and the same Spirit works all these things, distributing to each one individually as He wills. [12] For as the body is one and has many members, but all the members of that one body, being many, are one body, so also is Christ.*

The body of Christ - THE CHURCH, will continue to be malnourished if contempt for each other's unique abilities is nurtured. As men/women of God, we must learn to celebrate each other, embrace our diversity, and more importantly partner with each other in advancing the gospel of Christ.

## KINGDOM COMMUNITY

**IDENTITY DEFINES COMMUNITY.** As a man or woman of God, one of the factors that enable you fully maximize God's calling upon your life is your association. The call into ministry is not a call to be a lone ranger: God designed ministry to be carried out in communities through alliances and kingdom partnerships. The right relationships in ministry can positively impact on the success and fulfillment of your heavenly assignment while negative influences can deter, hinder, or destroy one's ministry. Oftentimes, the wrong community in ministry is largely a function of a lack of identity or false identity. Your community doesn't change until you discover your true identity. As it is said, "birds of the same feathers flock together".

> *Blessed is the man Who walks not in the counsel of the ungodly, nor stands in the path of sinners, nor sits in the seat of the scornful; But his delight is in the law of the LORD, And in His law he meditates day and night. He shall be like a tree Planted by the rivers of water, that brings forth its fruit in its season, whose leaf also shall not wither; And whatever he does shall prosper. The ungodly are not so but are like the chaff which the wind drives away.*

As kingdom officials, we do not choose our spiritual company based on our racial identity; we do by our kingdom identity. When this becomes the case, there will be no fear, no suspicion, or envy leading to contempt and condescending behaviors. What you are chosen by God to do has to influence the choice of your community because many have failed in life and ministry, not because of the wrong or evil they did, but because of the association they kept. Meanwhile, many others have greatly succeeded through the same power of association.

I must confess that I have been blessed by God all through my spiritual development and ministry journey with relationships that have shaped and helped me in my growth process and also challenged me to a higher standard as a man of God, for which I am truly grateful.

> *"Then it pleased the apostles and elders, with the whole church, to send chosen men of their own company to Antioch with Paul and Barnabas, namely, Judas who was also named Barsabas, and Silas, leading men among the brethren"*
> - Acts 15:22

Clearly, from the above scripture, the pursuit of kingdom agenda is not a business of just any and everybody. God operates through a chosen company, tribe, and covenant alliances; therefore, it is expedient that you find your spiritual company because therein lies the power of association. Note, the more you and I grow into our kingdom identity, the lesser our community grows. This is because not everyone will understand your God-given assignment. Some will, but the majority will not. It is impossible to incubate and hatch your vision amongst people who do not have a revelation of you or what God has called you to do.

The account of Joseph from the bible is a perfect case study of sharing your God-given vision with the wrong community of people. In Joseph's case, it was his brothers, which makes it even more painful that his dream killers were his own siblings. Therefore, we should not just build a community of everybody; we must prayerfully commit the building of our relationships to God for his help and guidance.

> *"God sets the solitary in families; He brings out those who are bound into prosperity; But the rebellious dwell in a dry land".*
> - Psalm 68:6 NKJV

# CHAPTER FOUR
# BEYOND THE NATURAL

*So Elijah answered and said to them, "If I am a man of God, let fire come down from heaven and consume you and your fifty men." And the fire of God came down from heaven and consumed him and his fifty.*

I have often said that faith and leadership are very similar in nature as they both are predicated on results. The lack of results invalidates the integrity of faith or leadership. A very important and truthful question we need to ask ourselves as men and women of God is this: of what relevance is a minister of the gospel, or a church, or ministry without tangible and undeniable manifestation of the power of God, especially in today's modern society where science and technology are attempting to explain away the existence of God? Like Gideon in the book of Judges (see Judges 6:13), the entire world is calling for the miracles we preach and proclaim as evidence that God truly exists. If you ever wondered why millennials and especially Gen Z generally find it difficult to respond to the faith life, much unlike other generations, I have an answer for you: it is simply because facts are not enough. This present generation of God-seekers wants proofs; they want evidence of what is true or proclaimed of this all-powerful God.

I recall from the book of Exodus, the first proof that Pharaoh demanded from Moses when he showed up with his claim that God had sent him to free the Israelites from him and their captivity in Egypt. Pharaoh requested a miracle from Moses as proof that God truly was involved in his rescue mission. Even Pharaoh, an idol worshipper, admitted that if God was truly involved, then there should be an element of supernatural manifestations of His power. As men and women of God, we can no longer afford to pursue kingdom defense or advancement without the miraculous or supernatural manifestation of God's power through our lives or ministries. We must go beyond the natural.

Elijah did not hesitate to demonstrate what it meant to be a man or woman of God when the captains of King Ahaziah came to arrest him. Elijah did not enter into debate with the king's troops: he immediately called down fire from heaven to defend himself and to prove the superiority of the kingdom he represented. To be a man or woman of God must mean more than the title; it must evidently show that God is involved in your life and ministry through supernatural manifestations or results.

In a time such as the one we currently are in, this is the standard we must maintain or attain by all scriptural means. Our ministerial position without the supernatural manifestations of the power of God will only be limited to intellectual debates and moral reasoning. While there is a place for these in defending and advancing the kingdom of God here on earth, however, we must realize we are not dealing with people. We are up against spiritual forces forged behind ideologies that can only be brought down through the power of God.

> *"For we do not wrestle against flesh and blood, but against principalities, against powers, against the rulers of the darkness of this age, against spiritual hosts of wickedness in the heavenly places".*
> *- Ephesians 6:12*

Jesus admitted this truth at some point in His own ministry, that His words without supernatural works may reflect as an inadequacy in His continuous attempt in defending and advancing His kingdom assignment here on earth.

> *"if you don't believe in the words that I speak, then believe in the works that I do"*

It is not that our words are unimportant to our positions or offices as men and women of God. In fact, the largest part of carrying out our ministry is through our words. So, the key element here is the fact that whatever is associated with some form of divinity is expected to be beyond the ordinary. This expectation either of spiritual things or people is not fundamentally based on cultural bias; rather, it stems from before any human being was created. God has been making Himself known through supernatural acts simply because He is a supernatural God.

This truth is the singular most viable explanation for why any Christian should not feel powerless and helpless. We carry this divine nature within us, and this gives us the ability to demonstrate the supernatural power that resides within this nature in us. I have no doubt in my spirit that God is calling us to raise the standard in this regard also; especially when this current generation is demanding for a real God, not just the talk of one.

My fear is that if we do not respond fast enough to this call, we will leave the body of Christ at further risk of abuse by false demonstration of supernatural power that is far from being the power of God. There have been too many incidences and news of abuse in Christendom lately due to the hunger of believers - especially young believers - to witness the tangible supernatural expression of God that has been preached for so long. Now that there is an awakening in the hearts of people, we have left the false men and women of God, Soothsayers, Psychics, and Astrologers to meet this need while we the true servants of God only want to elevate the corporate identity of the church.

## THE ROLES OF THE SUPERNATURAL

It is true that when the benefit of a thing is not known; then underutilization is inevitable. I believe that exploring the roles of the supernatural will further reveal the need and urgency of the supernatural in the life or ministry of a man or woman of God.

### PERSONAL VICTORIES

The miraculous power of God begins with our personal victories in every degree and ramification; right from the new birth, which I consider to be the greatest of all miracles. There are things going on in our lives that will linger on until the miracle force of God's power steps into those situations. Take the account of Apostle Peter into consideration: he was locked up in jail to be executed by King Herod, and miraculously broken free by the angel of the Lord. There would have been no other way for Peter's freedom without this supernatural prison break; which, had it not happened, would have resulted not only in the death of Peter but the end of a revival he spearheaded (See, Acts 12:5-11).

Just like Elijah, every man and woman of God including every born-again believer must desire to walk in the supernatural as our personal victories depend on it. The body of Christ is at war, and to defend ourselves, we will be required to position ourselves rightly in the power that is available to us in Christ. The battles of life that we fight either as men or women of God or as children of God can only be won victoriously through the supernatural power of God. Instead of reasoning everything happening to us, let us rather release our faith and believe God for miracles.

## TO MAKE OTHERS BELIEVE IN GOD

As Christian leaders, we are called and chosen by God to make believers. Miracles are like magnets; they draw people to God. We need to see many more miracles in the body of Christ today in order to see many more people come to the Lord. The entire world needs to experience the miracle-working power of God and we are the only opportunity for that to happen. The world we live in today is not so different from the days of Jesus Christ where it took consistent teaching of the word and the practical demonstration of the power of God for men to believe in God.

It took the supernatural resurrection of Lazarus from death, for the men in an entire city to believe in Jesus Christ. John recalls that it was on the account of him who had been raised from the dead that the men believed.

> *"Now a great many of the Jews knew that He was there; and they came, not for Jesus' sake only, but that they might also see Lazarus, whom He had raised from the dead. But the chief priests plotted to put Lazarus to death also, because on account of him many of the Jews went away and believed in Jesus."*
> *- John* 12:9-11

It can no longer be a case of pick-and-choose, but rather, it is expedient for men and women of God of today to assume this standard of supernatural demonstration of God's power available in the body of Christ. Otherwise, we stand the risk of becoming an object of reproach amongst the nations and spheres of society.

> *"Let the priests, who minister to the Lord, Weep between the porch and the altar; Let them say, "Spare Your people, O Lord, And do not give Your heritage to reproach, That the nations should rule over them. Why should they say among the peoples, 'Where is their God?"*
> – Joel 2:17

God forbid it, that our generation as men and women of God will be the cause of mockery to this sacred office of a man and woman of God. Elisha was deeply concerned when the dead son of the Shunamite woman didn't come back to life; first when his staff was laid on the boy's corpse, and when he himself went in to pray for the dead boy and nothing happened. But the Prophet didn't give up as two things were at stake here – the woman's faith and the prophet's credibility as a true man of God. After all, God is a great and mighty God whose power is limitless.

> *"And the mother of the child said, "As the Lord lives, and as your soul lives, I will not leave you." So, he arose and followed her. Now Gehazi went on ahead of them and laid the staff on the face of the child; but there was neither voice nor hearing. Therefore, he went back to meet him, and told him, saying, "The child has not awakened." When Elisha came into the house, there was the child, lying dead on his bed. He went in therefore, shut*

> *the door behind the two of them, and prayed to the Lord. And he went up and lay on the child, and put his mouth on his mouth, his eyes on his eyes, and his hands on his hands; and he stretched himself out on the child, and the flesh of the child became warm. He returned and walked back and forth in the house, and again went up and stretched himself out on him; then the child sneezed seven times, and the child opened his eyes."*
> – 2 Kings 4:30-36

Similar to Jesus (Acts 2:22), the early church in the days of the Apostles was characterized by several miraculous signs done by God through the Apostles, especially Paul to authenticate their calling as well as their ministry.

> "*And God wrought special miracles by the hands of Paul: So that from his body were brought unto the sick handkerchiefs or aprons, and the diseases departed from them, and the evil spirits went out of them.*"
> - Acts 19:11-12

Dear man or woman of God, the days of signs, wonders, and miracles are not in our past: those days are here right now. The times have never demanded the supernatural in bringing heaven's reality to earth's calamity more than now. You and I are responsible to make this happen, not yesterday, or tomorrow, but every day, till the entire world is filled with the knowledge of Christ's saving grace.

### TO DESTROY THE WORKS OF SATAN

It is important for us to know that Satan is also at work on the earth wreaking havoc and doing terrible things to God's creation. It will take the miraculous power of God in a lot of ways to undo what Satan is doing (See, Acts 10:38).

> "*He who sins is of the devil, for the devil has sinned from the beginning. For this purpose, the Son of God was manifested, that He might destroy the works of the devil*"
> - 1 *John* 3:8 NKJV

So many things we go through are forms of oppression from the devil and it will only take God's miraculous power to break free from these things (Mark 16:15-20, Acts 3:1-8). The Bible contains records of the blind receiving back their sight, the lame getting back their mobility, the dead raised back to life, and several others afflicted by the devil completely rescued and delivered from these various oppressions by the supernatural power of God that flows through the anointing.

> "*How God anointed Jesus of Nazareth with the Holy Spirit and with power, who went about*

*doing good and healing all who were oppressed by the devil, for God was with Him"*
- Acts 10:38 NKJV)

The good news is that Jesus gave every believer (Luke 10:17-19) power - Exousia in Greek (Delegated Authority - the right to use power as received and when needed to destroy Satan's works), to tread (to have absolute mastery) over serpents, scorpions, and all power of Satan. There is no doubt that God declared that you and I shall tread upon Satan (Psalm 91:13); but without the power to do so, it remains an impossible reality. Psalm 66:3 declares, **"*How awesome are Your works! Through the greatness of Your power, Your enemies shall submit themselves to You.*"** Hallelujah! Satan only bows to the power of God and it is to the degree of this power that is at work in your life as a man or woman of God, that Satan will submit to. Satan will successfully harass your destiny when your life is void of the power of God. Therefore, we must 'power up' daily!

## KINGDOM MOBILIZATION

*Your people shall be volunteers in the day of Your power; In the beauties of holiness, from the womb of the morning, You have the dew of Your youth.)*
*-Psalm 110:3*

No individual by himself or herself can successfully advance or promote the kingdom of God just by teaching and preaching it. God is raising an army of believers with tremendous power and exceptional abilities that will carry out this kingdom agenda. However, it will become difficult for any man or woman of God to accomplish this task of kingdom advancement without raising disciples who are baptized by the power of God. The manifestation of the power of God is what turns sinners into saints and makes ministers out of saints. In Acts 2:1, the same power of God made fearless and powerful Apostles out of fearful and intimidated disciples.

People will be more willing to engage in any form of kingdom service when they have encountered the supernatural power of God for themselves. Apostle Paul's tenacity and passion for kingdom advancement came out of his encounter with God and his transformation through the power of God. So, now we understand why Paul said, "He is not ashamed of the gospel, for it is the power of God unto salvation". Paul took the gospel of Jesus Christ far and wide, even at the risk of his own life because of what he knew and had experienced through the power of God.

The truth is that complacency becomes the culture where the power of God is not actively present nor engaged. This is the reason some churches that have not brought the balance to the 'POWER and WISDOM' of God will find it difficult to mobilize this current generation in service of the kingdom. Programs without a demonstration of the power of God are pointless in the pursuit of kingdom advancement.

> *"And being let go, they went to their own companions and reported all that the chief priests and elders had said to them. So, when they heard that, they raised their voice to God with one accord and said: "Lord, You are God, who made heaven and earth and the sea, and all that is in them, who by the mouth of Your servant David have said: 'Why did the nations rage, And the people plot vain things? The kings of the earth took their stand, And the rulers were gathered together Against the LORD and against His Christ.' "For truly against Your holy Servant Jesus, whom You anointed, both Herod and Pontius Pilate, with the Gentiles and the people of Israel, were gathered together to do whatever Your hand and Your purpose determined before to be done. Now, Lord, look on their threats, and grant to Your servants that with all boldness they may speak Your word, by stretching out Your hand to heal, and that signs and wonders may be done through the name of Your holy Servant Jesus." And when they had prayed, the place where they were assembled together was shaken; and they were*

*all filled with the Holy Spirit, and they spoke the word of God with boldness.*
- Acts 4:23-31

Again, scriptures such as Acts 10:38 and Isaiah 61:1-3 record that even Jesus was empowered for advancing the kingdom of God. If this is the case, all men and women of God, including our ministry teams, cannot afford to not continually grow in the power of God, in order to successfully continue the advancement of the kingdom of our God here on earth.

## NATIONAL TRANSFORMATION

National Reformation is a huge part of God's agenda and the supernatural plays a huge role in it. As men and women of God, we can longer step back from the political arena while Satan continues to manipulate our politics. God is not only interested in demonstrating his power in the church; He also wants to do the same in the government houses and the presidential villas. Otherwise, He will not instruct us to pray for those who are in political offices (1 Timothy 2:1-4). The power and the wisdom of God are the remedies for subverting the chaos the nations of the earth are going through right now.

As men and women of God, it is expedient that we turn to God (2 Chronicles 4:7) in prayers for our political leaders to come to a quick realization that we cannot replace God's wisdom with policies forged from the pit of hell and human ideologies rooted in the lust for power and pleasure. There are grave consequences when a nation turns its back on God, and this is currently what many political leaders are doing, not realizing the danger of Satan's terror that their respective nations have been exposed to as a result (Read, 2 Kings 7).

Frankly speaking, our communities, cities and even the entire nation is passing through several crises all at the same time. The truth is that many of the social ills that we currently are suffering from cannot be resolved by legislation: it will take the power and wisdom of God to bring change in smaller units and reformation at a national level. Dear man and woman of God, our cities, our states, and our countries need a miracle from God, and you are I are responsible for that to happen, or else, we ourselves have denied the power thereof.

> *"having a form of godliness but denying its power. And from such people turn away!"*
> - *2 Timothy* 3:5

In 2nd Kings chapter 2, when a crisis came up in the city that required a miraculous solution, Elisha the man of God rose to the occasion. In these present times, you and I must rise up like this man of God because the events of our times demand it.

> *Then the men of the city said to Elisha, "Please notice, the situation of this city is pleasant, as my lord sees; but the water is bad, and the ground barren." And he said, "Bring me a new bowl, and put salt in it." So, they brought it to him. Then he went out to the source of the water, and cast in the salt there, and said, "Thus says the LORD: 'I have healed this water; from it there shall be no more death or barrenness. So, the water remains healed to this day, according to the word of Elisha which he spoke."*
> *- 2 Kings 2:19-22*

## MIRACLE IN MODERN TIMES. HOW DOES IT WORK?

The question, 'do miracles still happen today?' is on so many lips across the vast culture of nations, especially in the western cultures. The Bible refers a lot to Babylon, a type of modern cities. It represents a civilization that relies on human strength and man's intellectual acumen, not on God's ability or wisdom. However, the study of the bible on Babylon-related subjects such as in the time of Daniel teaches how to live a victorious Christian life in our present modern-day world.

The truth is that the world is changing and will continue to do so but God does not change, and neither does His word. Every generation, regardless of its civilization, experiences its own evil in some form, and it can only be dealt with supernaturally. Technology has not relieved Satan of his job to kill, steal and destroy. In fact, in many ways, the advancement in our society has created more opportunities for the enemy to perpetuate his evil.

Today's ministers of God must open themselves up to innovations by the Spirit of God to have a cutting edge in leading ministries that will victoriously combat the devices of Satan in today's civilization.

The world we live in today is driven by radical enlightenment mostly rooted in worldly intellectualism that seeks to dismiss or scientifically explain away the existence of miracles today and in history; but all glory to Jesus, miracles are outlasting these arguments against them. Anyone can doubt what they are told, but it is difficult to doubt what you see and we have continued to witness the supernatural acts of God even in modern-day society.
The Premier Christian News published an article online on Thursday, December 22, 2022, titled:

'When miracles made the news in 2022'. Out of the three incidences reported about when Christians believed God did a miracle is one story recalled by the Deputy General Secretary of the Ukrainian Bible Society, who said that miracles were taking place in Ukraine, despite the horror of war.

In March, Anatoliy Raychynets, in Kyiv, reported that an increasing amount of people were turning to Christianity to find light in the darkness since the Russian invasion began. He said the power of God was preventing even worse devastation. He told Premier: "We are very grateful to all of you who are standing with us in prayer and solidarity. I want to tell you that with prayer we see so many miracles. I have personally seen many miracles over the last 16 days - when bombs or rockets have fallen but not exploded and lots of lives have been saved because of that. Russian tanks have been left because they were empty of fuel and soldiers have run off. In Odesa, in the Black Sea, there has been a storm for four days, and ships couldn't come closer to the city to shoot rockets. So, prayers are already bringing results and miracles are saving a lot of lives."

(To read more, https://premierchristian.news/us/news/article/when-miracles-made-the-news-in-2022).

As I said, the times will change, there will be an advancement in technology, wars will come and go, and new policies will be constituted and some abolished, but God will remain constant in all these changes. Essentially, this means that, regardless of the times, miracles will still exist!

As ministers of God, this must be our conviction, no matter what. We cannot stop believing God for the supernatural in and through our ministries, especially in dark times like this; otherwise, there will be no evidence that Jesus Christ is the same yesterday, today, and forever.

> *"Jesus Christ is the same yesterday, today, and forever."*
> *- Hebrews* 13:8 NKJV

# CHAPTER FIVE
# THE POWER OF PRAYER

*And the angel of the LORD said to Elijah, "Go down with him; do not be afraid of him." So, he arose and went down with him to the king.* 2 Kings 1:15 NKJV

Text: *Matthew* 16:19 NKJV

[19] And *I will give you the keys of the kingdom of heaven, and whatever you bind on earth will be bound in heaven, and whatever you loose on earth will be loosed in heaven."*

*Matthew* 16:19 TPT
[19] *I will give you the keys of heaven's kingdom realm to forbid on earth that which is forbidden in heaven, and to release on earth that which is released in heaven."*

Elijah was a man of prayer. As we see in the text, God communicated with him through an angel. Throughout the Bible, angels are seen to have been a divine response to the prayers directed to God by many Bible characters like David, Mary, Jacob, Paul, and even Jesus.

One of the keys to the kingdom of heaven that Jesus used all the time to forbid evil and release heaven on the earth is the KEY OF PRAYER. Prayer is a powerful weapon in the arsenal of God to resist the evil one in one's life and ministry.

> *And it happened when He was in a certain city, that behold, a man who was full of leprosy saw Jesus; and he fell on his face and implored Him, saying, "Lord, if You are willing, You can make me clean. "Then He put out His hand and touched him, saying, "I am willing; be cleansed." Immediately the leprosy left him. And He charged him to tell no one, "But go and show yourself to the priest, and make an offering for your cleansing, as a testimony to them, just as Moses commanded. "However, the report went around concerning Him more; and great multitudes came together to hear, and to be healed by Him of their infirmities. So, He Himself often withdrew into the wilderness and prayed.*
> - Luke 5:12-16 NKJV

A believer or minister without an active prayer life is subject to mockery and satanic molestation. Prayer is the power system of the kingdom that lights up the church of Jesus Christ and the life of a believer. Any minister of God without a dedicated prayer life runs the risk of being in the kingdom but never having a taste of the wonders of this kingdom. Jesus had such a phenomenal prayer lifestyle that was so enviable to the point that His d so desired to have that kind of prayer life.

> *Now it came to pass, as He was praying in a certain place, when He ceased, that one of His disciples said to Him, "Lord, teach us to pray, as John also taught his disciples."*
> - *Luke* 11:1 NKJV

The greatest gift of spiritual leadership to you and me is to be taught how to pray, and you as a man or woman of God must also teach those that you lead; otherwise, your ministry team will be powerless and easily molested by Satan. The one who knows how to pray will never again be defeated by the devil. Jesus prayed all the time – TO FORBID AND TO RELEASE – and every born-again Christian must develop this kind of prayer life.

*And it happened when He was in a certain city, that behold, a man who was full of leprosy saw Jesus; and he fell on his face and implored Him, saying, "Lord, if You are willing, You can make me clean. Then He put out His hand and touched him, saying, "I am willing; be cleansed." Immediately the leprosy left him. And He charged him to tell no one, But go and show yourself to the priest, and make an offering for your cleansing, as a testimony to them, just as Moses commanded. However, the report went around concerning Him more; and great multitudes came together to hear, and to be healed by Him of their infirmities. So, He Himself often withdrew into the wilderness and prayed."*

- *Luke* 5:12-16 NKJV

An important reason prayer is powerful and important not only to ministers of the gospel but to every Christian is that prayer is consent. It is giving God the legal right to supernaturally interfere and intervene in all our personal affairs or matters of the earth, thereby establishing His supremacy and Lordship over evil and all as we read in the case of Elijah.

*May you be blessed by the* LORD, *Who made heaven and earth. The heaven, even the heavens, are the* LORD's; *But the earth He has given to the children of men.*
- *Psalm* 115:15-16 NKJV

For God to do anything on the earth, an agreement is required, and we enter into this agreement through prayer; which is why, in the kingdom, the PRAYER OF AGREEMENT is POWERFUL.

"Assuredly, I *say to you, whatever you bind on earth will be bound in heaven, and whatever you loose on earth will be loosed in heaven.* "Again, I *say to you that if two of you agree on earth concerning anything that they ask, it will be done for them by* My *Father in heaven. For where two or three are gathered together in* My *name,* I *am there in the midst of them.*"
- *Matthew* 18:18-20 NKJV

Let us see how it reads in The Passion Translation:

"Receive *this truth:* Whatever *you forbid on earth will be considered to be forbidden in heaven, and whatever you release on earth will be considered to be released in heaven.* Again, I *give you an eternal truth:* If *two of you agree to ask* God *for something in a symphony of prayer, my heavenly* Father *will do it for you.* For *wherever two or*

*three come together in honor of my name, I am right there with them!"*
- *Matthew* 18:18-20 TPT

Praying with the word is the same as agreeing with the word; which means you are giving consent to God to intervene in your life or ministry situations. Your only guarantee that your prayers will be answered is when your prayers align with the will of the Lord as revealed, spoken, or written in His Word. The real beauty of prayer begins to unfold when prayer becomes a lifestyle: that is when the different aspects of prayer are revealed to you, such as the Prayer of Devotion, Prayer of Petition, Prayer of Supplication, Prayer of Intercession, Prayer of Reconciliation, and Prayer for the Nation.

All these are different approaches to prayer that I recommend you study through the word of God to make prayer more productive and for effective ministry. Let us briefly highlight a few benefits of prayer.

## BENEFITS OF PRAYER

### DELIVERANCE FROM SATANIC AFFLICTION:

Prayer is the key to breaking free from any type of demonic attack or stronghold. Jesus prayed for Peter against the attack of Satan.

> *"But this kind of demon is cast out only through prayer and fasting."* - *Matthew* 17:21 TPT

> *"Are there any believers in your fellowship suffering great hardship and distress? Encourage them to pray! Are there happy, cheerful ones among you? Encourage them to sing out their praises! Are there any sick among you? Then ask the elders of the church to come and pray over the sick and anoint them with oil in the name of our Lord. And the prayer of faith will heal the sick and the Lord will raise them up, and if they have committed sins they will be forgiven".*
> - *James* 5:13-15 TPT

### SPIRITUAL ENLIGHTENMENT:

The benefits of the kingdom are only accessible by revelation. Without revelation, you and I will continue to struggle to make the most of this kingdom citizenship.

*"Call to Me, and I will answer you, and show you great and mighty things, which you do not know."*
- *Jeremiah* 33:3 NKJV

*"And Elisha prayed, and said,* "LORD, *I pray, open his eyes that he may see."* Then *the* LORD *opened the eyes of the young man, and he saw. And behold, the mountain was full of horses and chariots of fire all around Elisha.* So, *when the Syrians came down to him, Elisha prayed to the* LORD, *and said,* "Strike *this people, I pray, with blindness."* And *He struck them with blindness according to the word of* Elisha."
- 2 *Kings* 6:17-18 NKJV

"Therefore *I also, after I heard of your faith in the* Lord Jesus *and your love for all the saints, do not cease to give thanks for you, making mention of you in my prayers:* that the God *of our* Lord Jesus Christ, *the* Father *of glory, may give to you the spirit of wisdom and revelation in the knowledge of* Him, *the eyes of your understanding being enlightened; that you may know what is the hope of* His *calling, what are the riches of the glory of* His *inheritance in the saints, and what is the exceeding greatness of* His *power toward us who believe, according to the working of* His *mighty power."*
- Ephesians 1:15-19 NKJV

**OPEN HEAVENS:**

For a believer, an open heaven is non-negotiable or excusable, especially if you and I want to experience the BLESSINGS OF THE LORD in our lives or in what we do.

> "The LORD *will open to you* His *good treasure, the heavens, to give the rain to your land in its season, and to bless all the work of your hand.* You *shall lend to many nations, but you shall not borrow."*
> - *Deuteronomy* 28:12 NKJV

There are two things the bible records that open heaven over a believer's life: PRAYER & GIVING.

> "When *all the people were baptized, it came to pass that* Jesus *also was baptized; and while* He *prayed, the heaven was opened.* And *the* Holy Spirit *descended in bodily form like a dove upon* Him, *and a voice came from heaven which said,* "You *are* My *beloved* Son; *in* You I *am well pleased."*
> - *Luke* 3:21-22 NKJV

> "*Bring all the tithes into the storehouse,* That *there may be food in* My *house,* And *try* Me *now in this,"* Says *the* LORD *of hosts,* "*If* I *will not open for you the windows of heaven and pour out for you*

*such blessing That there will not be room enough to receive it."*
- *Malachi* 3:10 NKJV

*"There was a certain man in Caesarea called Cornelius, a centurion of what was called the Italian Regiment, a devout man and one who feared God with all his household, who gave alms generously to the people, and prayed to God always. About the ninth hour of the day, he saw clearly in a vision an angel of God coming in and saying to him, "Cornelius!" [4] And when he observed him, he was afraid, and said, "What is it, lord?" So, he said to him, "Your prayers and your alms have come up for a memorial before God. Now send men to Joppa and send for Simon whose surname is Peter. He is lodging with Simon, a tanner, whose house is by the sea. He will tell you what you must do. "And when the angel who spoke to him had departed, Cornelius called two of his household servants and a devout soldier from among those who waited on him continually. So, when he had explained all these things to them, he sent them to Joppa. The next day, as they went on their journey and drew near the city, Peter went up on the housetop to pray, about the sixth hour. Then he became very hungry and wanted to eat; but while they made ready, he fell into a trance and saw heaven opened and an object like a great*

*sheet bound at the four corners, descending to him, and let down to the earth."*
- Acts 10:1-11,38 NKJV

**TO UNLOCK THE SUPERNATURAL:**
Without the supernatural, we have no authentic claim on Christianity. The supernatural dimension was what caused people to refer to the early believers as 'Christians' and it was because they prayed non-stop. The supernatural is not based on ordination but on supplication: this is why you do not need to be ordained to walk in the supernatural, you just need to be PRAYED-UP!

*"Elijah was a man with a nature like ours, and he prayed earnestly that it would not rain; and it did not rain on the land for three years and six months. And he prayed again, and the heaven gave rain, and the earth produced its fruit."*
- James 5:17-18 NKJV

*"Elijah was a man with human frailties, just like all of us, but he prayed and received supernatural answers. He shut the heavens over the land so there would be no rain for three and a half years! Then he prayed again, and the skies opened over the land so that the rain came again and produced the harvest."*
- James 5:17-18 TPT

## TWO METHODS OF PRAYER

**PERSONAL PRAYER:**

No one knows the battle you are fighting better than you do, therefore you are better off praying about your issues. That is why the scripture says you should come boldly to the throne of grace.

> *"And Jabez called on the God of Israel saying, "Oh, that You would bless me indeed, and enlarge my territory, that Your hand would be with me, and that You would keep me from evil, that I may not cause pain!"* So, *God granted him what he requested."*
>
> - 1 *Chronicles* 4:10 NKJV

All destiny-related issues are matters of prayer and thus require personal responsibility. Many of the people that say I'm praying for you are lying; they are not. Go ask Jesus!

> *Then Jesus came with them to a place called Gethsemane, and said to the disciples, "Sit here while I go and pray over there. "And He took with Him Peter and the two sons of Zebedee, and He began to be sorrowful and deeply distressed. Then He said to them, "My soul is exceedingly sorrowful, even to death. Stay here and watch with Me." He went a little farther and fell on His*

*face, and prayed, saying, "O My Father, if it is possible, let this cup pass from Me; nevertheless, not as I will, but as You will." Then He came to the disciples and found them sleeping, and said to Peter, "What! Could you not watch with Me one hour? Watch and pray, lest you enter into temptation. The spirit indeed is willing, but the flesh is weak." Again, a second time, He went away and prayed, saying, "O My Father, if this cup cannot pass away from Me unless I drink it, Your will be done. "And He came and found them asleep again, for their eyes were heavy. So, He left them, went away again, and prayed the third time, saying the same words. Then He came to His disciples and said to them, "Are you still sleeping and resting? Behold, the hour is at hand, and the Son of Man is being betrayed into the hands of sinners. Rise, let us be going. See, My betrayer is at hand." - Matthew* 26:36-46 NKJV

**CORPORATE PRAYER:**
From the very first church planted by the Apostles of Christ until this present-day church, the most powerful kingdom-influencing churches, and ministries are the ones given to an undying commitment to corporate prayer. There is tremendous power generated in corporate prayer meetings. Let us look at this time when the early church came together to pray for Peter.

*"Now about that time Herod the king stretched out his hand to harass some from the church. Then he killed James the brother of John with the sword. And because he saw that it pleased the Jews, he proceeded further to seize Peter also. Now it was during the Days of Unleavened Bread. So, when he had arrested him, he put him in prison, and delivered him to four squads of soldiers to keep him, intending to bring him before the people after Passover. Peter was therefore kept in prison, but constant prayer was offered to God for him by the church. And when Herod was about to bring him out, that night Peter was sleeping, bound with two chains between two soldiers; and the guards before the door were keeping the prison. Now behold, an angel of the Lord stood by him, and a light shone in the prison; and he struck Peter on the side and raised him up, saying, "Arise quickly!" And his chains fell off his hands. Then the angel said to him, "Gird yourself and tie on your sandals"; and so, he did. And he said to him, "Put on your garment and follow me." So, he went out and followed him, and did not know that what was done by the angel was real, but thought he was seeing a vision. When they were past the first and the second guard posts, they came to the iron gate that leads to the city, which opened to them of its own accord; and they went out and went down one street, and immediately the angel*

*departed from him. And when Peter had come to himself, he said, Now I know for certain that the Lord has sent His angel and has delivered me from the hand of Herod and from all the expectation of the Jewish people." So, when he had considered this, he came to the house of Mary, the mother of John whose surname was Mark, where many were gathered praying. And as Peter knocked at the door of the gate, a girl named Rhoda came to answer. When she recognized Peter's voice, because of her gladness she did not open the gate, but ran in and announced that Peter stood before the gate."*
- Acts 12:1-14 NKJV

A praying church is a triumphant church in all matters and affairs of kingdom expansion here on earth. Corporate prayer meetings are not old-fashioned; they are the power-generating source of a church or ministry. The level of power generated by corporate meetings is unmatched if it becomes a consistent practice by a church or ministry. God does not only delight in our corporate prayers, but He moves swiftly in response to our corporate prayers.

*"If My people who are called by My name will humble themselves, and pray and seek My face, and turn from their wicked ways, then I will hear*

*from heaven, and will forgive their sin and heal their land."*
- *2 Chronicles* 7:14 NKJV

Pastors and ministry leaders, we must be very careful not to turn our intercessory team into prayer contractors. An important role of the intercessory team is to be prayer initiators to spark up the desire and an awakening for corporate prayer within the church or your ministry.

## HOW SHOULD WE PRAY

**With Fervency:**
There is a dynamic force that rends the heaven that is generated through passionate heartfelt prayer.

*He prayed even more passionately, like one being sacrificed, until he was in such intense agony of spirit that his sweat became drops of blood, dripping onto the ground."*
- *Luke* 22:44 TPT

*Epaphras, who is one of you, a bondservant of Christ, greets you, always laboring fervently for you in prayers, that you may stand perfect and complete in all the will of God."*
- Colossians 4:12 NKJV

*"Confess your trespasses to one another, and pray for one another, that you may be healed. The effective, fervent prayer of a righteous man avails much."*
- James 5:16 NKJV

**WITH BOLDNESS:**
Timidity in the place of prayer is a major hindrance to effectiveness in prayer. We are not praying as victims but as VICTORS!

*"Seeing then that we have a great High Priest who has passed through the heavens, Jesus the Son of God, let us hold fast our confession. [15] For we do not have a High Priest who cannot sympathize with our weaknesses, but was in all points tempted as we are, yet without sin. [16] Let us therefore come boldly to the throne of grace, that we may obtain mercy and find grace to help in time of need."*
- Hebrews 4:14-16 NKJV

*"So we may boldly say: "The LORD is my helper; I will not fear. What can man do to me?"*
*- Hebrews* 13:6 NKJV

**IN THE SPIRIT:**

Praying in the Spirit is crucial for the accuracy of prayer, otherwise, your prayer will not hit any target.

*"And if you ask, you won't receive it for you're asking with corrupt motives, seeking only to fulfil your own selfish desires."*
*- James* 4:3 TPT

*"Likewise, the Spirit also helps in our weaknesses. For we do not know what we should pray for as we ought, but the Spirit Himself makes intercession for us with groanings which cannot be uttered. Now He who searches the hearts knows what the mind of the Spirit is, because He makes intercession for the saints according to the will of God."*
*- Romans* 8:26-27 NKJV

Prophetically, I believe that God will immerse the church of today again in His word and a fresh baptism of GRACE FOR FERVENCY OF PRAYER. However, the longing for this must begin at the altar not just at the pews. Men and women of God must return from ministry activity to spiritual intensity.

> *"And I will pour on the house of David and on the inhabitants of Jerusalem the Spirit of grace and supplication; then they will look on Me whom they pierced. Yes, they will mourn for Him as one mourns for his only son and grieve for Him as one grieves for a firstborn."*
> \- *Zechariah* 12:10 NKJV

# CHAPTER SIX
# THE MERCY OF GOD

*Again, he sent a third captain of fifty with his fifty men. And the third captain of fifty went up, and came and fell on his knees before Elijah, and pleaded with him, and said to him: "Man of God, please let my life and the life of these fifty servants of yours be precious in your sight.*

There is little or no room for biases, either conscious or unconscious, in our present world of cultural diversity and division, racial tension and inequality, and political differences and indifferences. The level of pain and number of disgruntled individuals in our nations today is unfathomable, making it an urgent necessity to be much more considerate in dealing with people as men and women of God.  To demonstrate the level of consideration that will unite and heal, we must first deal with our prejudices and heal from our pains. Our defense and advancement of the kingdom of God have remained ineffective because of our woundedness, pain, bitterness, lack of trust, unforgiveness, and stereotypes stemming from prejudice.

Largely, an important aspect of the church's apostolic mandate is to execute righteousness in the place of unrighteousness, which is impossible without the honest demonstration of the mercy of God. Redemption power flows through the graciousness and the mercifulness of God.

> *"Or do you despise the riches of His goodness, forbearance, and longsuffering, not knowing that the goodness of God leads you to repentance?"*
> - *Romans* 2:4

The Bible is consistent in revealing that God is gracious and merciful. He is not easily angered; full of kindness, and anxious not to punish us (Joel 2:13). Therefore, if we are His ministers, we also must be merciful in deploying the ministry of our Lord Jesus Christ, otherwise we will make it difficult for both the saved and the unsaved to encounter the riches of God grace.

> *But You, O Lord, are a God full of compassion, and gracious, Longsuffering and abundant in mercy and truth.*
> - *Psalm* 86:15

As a man or woman of God, despite the people, nation, or world system coming against you or your ministry (just like in the case of Elijah), we cannot move outside of the mercy of God. Inasmuch as the king did not give up on sending his troops against Elijah, and God granted him the supernatural ability to overcome them, still God required Elijah to be merciful and gracious towards the captain and his troops (see, 2nd Kings 1:13-15). In Matthew chapter 26, when Jesus was being arrested, he behaved differently from his disciple, Peter. Jesus could have done what Elijah did; calling down fire to consume the army sent against him 10 times more powerful than Elijah, but He didn't. Jesus went as far as healing the perpetrator whose ear Peter had chopped off without hesitation in defense of Jesus Christ. Like Peter, we are required to be passionate for the cause of the kingdom of God, as Peter's approach to defending the kingdom was through condemnation which will not lead to redemption. The Spirit of the Lord revealed to me that the reason why many have rejected Jesus and the message of His kingdom is because our actions contradict this loving and merciful God we preach through our sermons!

Honestly, my attempt in writing this book is not to posture perfection, neither is my effort to deny or excuse the pain we have all had to endure in ministry. A lot of us have been wounded in the most despicable ways possible, and the truth is that God feels our pain and wants to help us heal as He has helped me to heal and get restored. But this cannot happen until we are willing to let go of our position and assume the right posture before the Lord that allows Him to move in our lives and ministries. As men and women of God, the grace and mercy of God can only begin to flow from us when we let go of our pain and prejudice, no matter how deep or how long the pain has lasted.

The man of God, Ananias was challenged by God to this very standard of spiritual leadership. Due to Ananias's past pain of Saul's persecution against the believers, his prejudice against Paul hindered him from seeing what was soon to become a major revival in the history of Christianity of his time. This was something that God Himself was personally spearheading through Saul, whom God had converted and renamed Paul - an Apostle per excellence. Paul's ministry is still today considered as one of the most powerful kingdom-advancing and kingdom-defending ministries of the New Testament church to ever exist. The truth is this: the lack of mercy and grace is rendering our evangelism non-effective in reaching lost souls in our present day. Like Ananias, we have judged outside of the mercy and graciousness of God, so it has become difficult for the love of Jesus Christ to be experienced through our ministry.

As a man or woman of God, it is crucial to understand this truth: that without the mercy of God, grace is hindered; and without the flow of grace, redemption is inaccessible. A man or woman of God must be quick to forgive, refusing to allow Satan to capitalize on our pain or disappointment. This will require a level of vulnerability that is difficult, especially for we frontline ministers; but when we consider Jesus Christ according to Philippians chapter 2, who, being equal to God, according to scriptures, did not demand nor cling to His right as God, we see a worthy pattern to follow. Jesus laid aside his deity, taking the disguise of a slave and becoming like men, and humbled Himself even further, going as far as dying a criminal's death on a cross! Let us find strength in His example to stand as true kingdom representatives here on earth.

The anger of Moses towards the irresponsibility of the people he led out of slavery hindered him from fulfilling his assignment and entering the promised land. What a cost! Pain from present or past hurts and resentment from prejudices are destiny killers, especially for a man or woman of God. I decided early as a minister of God, that with the help of the Holy Spirit, I will not have my heart tainted by past, present, and future hurt or unresolved pain. As a man or woman of God, it is inevitable not to be offended as long as we are in service to God, but we do not have to live with the bitterness of offenses. Like myself, I encourage you to guard your heart against unresolved offense. Do not allow the pain of offense to hinder your walk with God.

Several years ago, the Holy Spirit led me to study the entire book of First and Second Samuel with a keen focus on the life of David, especially his betrayal from King Saul. Through this study, I discovered the depth of mercifulness that David demonstrated towards King Saul and others who brought severe pain to his life, even to the point of making several attempts on his life. I also noticed David's disposition towards the demise of some of these individuals who committed all manner of atrocities against him. On some occasions, David even mourned and would refuse to eat at the news of the death of his enemies. What a heart of mercy that he had; no wonder God called him a man after His own heart!

David practically demonstrated what Jesus admonished His disciples (including us) in Luke 6:27-29. Jesus said ***"But I say to you who hear: Love your enemies, do good to those who hate you, bless those who curse you, and pray for those who spitefully use you. To him who strikes you on the one cheek, offer the other also. And from him who takes away your cloak, do not withhold your tunic either."*** This right here is a true reflection of our heavenly Father's heart; a heart full of compassion and mercy and as His representatives, this should also be our disposition even when it hurts.

## DEALING WITH PAIN, PREJUDICE & PRIDE

Pain is something all of us, regardless of our ministerial or social status, will experience: but how we respond or handle it is what reflects how much of the Christ-nature we have allowed the Holy Spirit to work in and through us. Pain is not a sinful emotional reaction, but what is not pleasing to God - especially as ministers of God - is any negative behavior or reaction that is used to express or resolve our displeasure for a wrong done to us.

In the moment of anger, you must not only remember that you hold an esteemed position as a representative of God but more importantly, remember God's standard for conducting yourself as a man or woman of God based on the scripture: "to be angry and sin not."

> *"Be angry, and do not sin. Meditate within your heart on your bed, and be still. Selah"*
> *- Psalms* 4:4 NKJV

In dealing with pain of any sort, we must give it to the Lord, surrendering our emotions to Him in the place of prayer. Letting go of our negative emotions to the Lord is the healthiest way to handle the feeling of pain. The Apostle Peter, admonishing the believer, said emphatically: ***"Cast all your anxiety on him because he cares for you"*** (1 Peter 5:7 NIV). In releasing the feeling of pain to the Lord, you must be completely honest with your feelings, admit your inability to handle them, revoke your right to revenge, and trust Him to be your defender.

The lie of the devil is that when an offense is committed against you, you have the right to hurt back. This is what makes it difficult for you to release the pain to the Lord. Sadly, as ministers of the gospel, and even as Christians, you and I do not have that right or privilege to hurt back. No level of pain will ever give us the right to retaliate; the power we will be given in this painful process is to give to the Lord.

The Lord says, "'It is mine to avenge; I will repay'" (Romans 12:19 NIV). He wants us to trust Him to set things right and even the score. When we surrender our anger, we may still feel hurt, but that hurt won't express itself in active or passive retaliation.

> *"My fellow believers, do not practice your faith in our glorious Lord Jesus Christ with an attitude of partiality [toward people-show no favoritism, no prejudice, no snobbery]." - James 2:1* AMP

> *If, however, you are [really] fulfilling the royal law according to the Scripture,* "YOU SHALL LOVE YOUR NEIGHBOR AS YOURSELF *[that is, if you have an unselfish concern for others and do things for their benefit]" you are doing well. But if you show partiality [prejudice, favoritism], you are committing sin and are convicted by the Law as offenders."*
> *- James 2:8-9* AMP

In as much as Elijah had the right to defend himself, he was also quick to obey the voice of the Lord to spare the troops sent to arrest him. The Bible also says that the anger of the Lord is but for a moment; which means that we as ministers must also be very quick to show the mercy of God, especially given the truth that we too have been shown tremendous mercy by the Lord.

Let us not allow pride to prevent us from admitting that there may still be pain that we are harboring deep down in our hearts from past hurts, that still affect the way to deal with people in our present. Sometimes we do not realize that this pain comes from hate stories unknowingly passed down to us from either our parents or members of our family. These feelings do not just go away simply because we grow up or we find our calling in Christ. Pain, pride, or any form of prejudice must be surrendered to God. Only in Christ can we find our healing and complete deliverance from the psychological torture and emotional horror of the demon called GRUDGE.

Clinically, it has been proven that holding a grudge for a wrong done to you such as a false accusation, betrayal, childhood bullying, or another person stealing the credit for your accomplishment will only hurt you. In an analysis by van Monsjou, E., Struthers, C. W., Fergus, K., & Muise, A. (2021) Examining the lived experience of holding grudges. Qualitative Psychology. Advance online publication of 20 interviews conducted, it is reported that grudges may foster feelings of moral superiority and prove difficult to let go of. More importantly, they can negatively affect your quality of life. For instance, they may lead you to seek validation (especially in the wrong places. Emphasis is mine), cut ties with others, or shape your expectation for the future.

In my conclusion, this should not be your story. You do not have to bear the weight of ministry and at the same time, carry the unnecessary weight of past hurts. It is my prayer that you will find the strength and fortitude to surrender control to God and let Him bear your pain, and in return, give you the peace and joy you deserve in Jesus's name, Amen!

# MY PRAYER FOR YOUR MINISTRY

*But you be watchful in all things, endure afflictions, do the work of an evangelist, fulfill your ministry.*
- 2 *Timothy* 4:5 NKJV

Dear Minister, it is my hope and prayer that this book has been of some help to you as you continue to navigate challenging terrain of ministry. I come in agreement with you that you will not fail in fulfilling your ministry. Your ministry will bear fruits of the kingdom; fruits that will outlive you for the sake of posterity. I pray that your ministry will not lack the necessary resources to fulfil its mandate and vision. I pray the Lord assign helpers to your ministry and prosper them under your covering. I pray that you will enjoy sound health and healing where healing is needed. Your household is preserved and blessed admis the chaos all around; no evil will penetrate your walls. I pray only peace and prosperity shall be found within your walls. Enjoy increase and enlargement. May your life and work for the Lord bring honor and glory to His name now and forevermore in Jesus's name, Amen!

I will see you at the top!

# Reflection Notes

## Reflection Notes

# Reflection Notes

## Reflection Notes

# Reflection Notes

# Reflection Notes

## Reflection Notes

# Reflection Notes

## Reflection Notes

If you would like to share a testimony or your experience while reading this book, please email the author at info@eagleworldoutreach.org

*To stay connected with Femi Adun:*
*Twitter*: @femiadun
*Instagram:* @femiadun
*Facebook*: @femiadun
*TikTok*: @femiadun

*Visit:* www.eagleworldoutreach.org

www.ingramcontent.com/pod-product-compliance
Lightning Source LLC
LaVergne TN
LVHW091033150826
845672LV00006BA/1792

* 9 7 8 1 7 3 9 7 0 0 9 6 6 *